Curriculum Visions

Christian

days

Northamptonshire
DISCARDED
Libraries

Please return/renew this item by the last date
shown. Books may be renewed by
telephoning, writing to or calling in at any
library or on the Internet.

Northamptonshire Libraries and Information Service

Northamptonshire
County Council

www.northamptonshire.gov.uk/leisure/libraries/

80 002 717 213

The ceremony of Holy Communion.

Glossary

ADVENT A word which means 'coming', or the arrival of something that has been waited for, such as the coming of Jesus. It is the period of four weeks which lead up to Christmas.

BAPTISM A ritual in which a person is welcomed into the Christian church. It involves having water poured onto the head, or immersion in water. The water stands for rebirth, and during baptism a person is reborn into the Christian church. In some traditions a person is baptised shortly after birth while in others people choose to be baptised as adults.

CENSUS A counting of all the people in a certain country or place. Censuses are an important way for leaders to find out how many people are living in their country so they can plan how to tax them and care for them.

CRUCIFIXION A way that the ancient Romans used to kill criminals by nailing or tying them to a cross.

DISCIPLE A follower. This word is usually used to describe a close follower of a religious leader, such as Jesus. Jesus' disciples are also called the Apostles.

EMMANUEL A Hebrew name meaning, 'God is with us'.

EPIPHANY Also called the twelfth day of Christmas. This celebrates the day, 12 days after Jesus was born, when the wise men arrived in Bethlehem to proclaim Jesus as the Messiah.

HOLY COMMUNION A worship ritual where worshippers share bread and wine as a reminder of Jesus' last supper with his disciples. This ritual is also called the Eucharist, or Mass.

HOLY SPIRIT The way in which God acts on Earth. During the life of Jesus people saw, heard and touched him. The Holy Spirit cannot be seen, heard or touched, but Christians believe they can see the work of the Holy Spirit in the effects of the Holy Spirit's actions on what we can actually see.

JESUS CHRIST The Son of God and the Messiah. The part of God that lived on Earth. The word Christ comes from the Greek word 'christos' meaning 'anointed one'.

LAST SUPPER The last meal that Jesus shared with his disciples. It was a Passover meal.

MANGER A trough or an open box in which feed for livestock is placed.

NATIVITY PLAY A play or show which tells the story of Jesus' birth. Nativity means 'birth'. Nativity plays are usually put on during Advent at Christmas.

ORTHODOX A Christian tradition which is practised in many countries such as Russia and Greece. It is the oldest Christian tradition.

PASSION PLAY A play which tells the story of Easter. This is also called the Passion of Christ. When used this way, the word passion means 'suffering'. So, a passion play tells the story of Christ's suffering. Most passion plays tell the story from the day Jesus arrived in Jerusalem until his death on the cross.

REPENT/PENITENCE To express sorrow for doing something bad and to try and make up for it with prayers and by doing good things.

RESURRECTION Bringing back from the dead. God brought Jesus back from the dead after his crucifixion.

SABBATH Another word for a day of worship. Sunday is the Christian sabbath.

SAVIOUR Another way of describing Jesus. A saviour is someone who rescues or 'saves' another person. Christians believe that Jesus was sent to save people from their sins, so he is called 'the Saviour'.

SEASON In the Christian faith, the year is divided up into seasons or holy times. Each season may last a few days or a few months and may contain one or more holy days.

Contents

As you go through the book, look for words in **BOLD CAPITALS**. These words are defined in the glossary.

⚠ Understanding others

Remember that other people's beliefs are important to them. You must always be considerate and understanding when studying about faith.

Christmas carols and a Christmas tree.

What is a holy day?

Christian holidays celebrate important events in the life of Jesus Christ.

People of all faiths worship throughout the whole year. But in all faiths, some days are special. These special days, or holy days, may remember an important event in the history of the faith, or they may be written about in holy writings, or scripture.

These holy days are different from a day of rest and worship that many religions have each week. Many holy days involve public celebrations, special meals, festivals and even processions. In general, we call these special days holy days and it is from this that we get the word 'holiday'.

In the Christian faith, the weekly day of rest is called the SABBATH and is on Sunday. But there are many holy days and times throughout the year, each with its own name. These days and times celebrate or remember important events in the life of JESUS CHRIST and his DISCIPLES.

The Christian Church divides the holy year up into SEASONS. Each season has one or more holy days. For example, the church season of Christmas lasts for 12 days and includes the holy days of Christmas and St Stephen's day.

▲▶ Christmas day is a happy and joyous time when many people celebrate the birth of Jesus with a big meal with friends and family. Other holy days may be more solemn times to remember and reflect (inset).

As you look at the main seasons and holy days of the Christian faith in this book, notice how each day is marked out or celebrated in a different way. Some holy days remember Jesus' life and teachings, while others remember Jesus' death and resurrection, and still others remember events that happened to Jesus' disciples. So, some of these holy days are happy and joyous times, and others are times to be solemn and reflective.

Weblink: www.CurriculumVisions.com

The Christian holy day calendar

**Here are the parts of the year when Christian holy days occur.
The actual dates of some of the holidays vary from one year to another.**

To keep track of the days of the year, many people in the world use a calendar which divides the year into 12 months and begins on January 1. In this calendar, the Sun is used as a guide and one year is about the time it takes the Earth to move around the Sun.

▲ Singing in church and in the community is an important part of many Christian holy days.

But not all calendars look like this. Some calendars, for example, use the way the Moon moves across the sky as a guide. Some of these calendars add an extra month every two or three years. So, the holy days move around a little each year. This is how the Jewish calendar works.

When Christianity began, it used the Jewish calendar. Later, the calendar was changed, but some of the holy days on the Christian calendar still move around a little each year.

The common calendar we use today is called the Gregorian calendar. It was begun in 1582 and named after Pope Gregory XIII (1502–1585). Before that another calendar, called the Julian calendar (begun by Julius Caesar) was used. Some Christian Churches, such as the Eastern **ORTHODOX** Church, still use the Julian calendar. The two calendars are not exactly the same and this is why some Christian Churches celebrate holidays on different dates.

▶ In this chart, you can see how the Christian holy days are spread around the year. You can also see how some of the holidays move around a little from year to year.

CHRISTIAN HOLY DAYS

▲ Easter vigil in an Orthodox church.

	2007	**2008**	**2009**	**2010**	**2011**
Advent begins	Dec 3 2006	Dec 2 2007	Nov 30 2008	Nov 29 2009	Nov 28 2010
Lent begins	Feb 21	Feb 6	Feb 25	Feb 17	March 9
Easter	April 8	March 23	April 12	April 4	April 24
Pentecost	May 27	May 11	May 31	May 23	June 12
Harvest festival*	Varies from church to church				
Christmas	Dec 25	Dec 25	Dec 25	Dec 25	Dec 25

*Harvest festivals are traditionally held on or near the Sunday of the Harvest Moon. This Moon is the Full Moon which falls in the month of September, at or around the time of the autumnal equinox, about Sept 23.

Weblink: www.CurriculumVisions.com

The holy time of Advent

This is a holy time of preparation before the Christmas holiday.

We usually think of holidays as lasting one or two days. But some Christian holidays last for many weeks. For example, the Christian calendar begins with a holy time called **ADVENT** that lasts for 40 days (starting on the fourth Sunday before December 25). Advent ends with the holy day of Christmas.

Advent is a time when Christians get ready to celebrate Christmas. One way that they do this is by learning the story of Christmas, which tells of the birth of Jesus.

▶ An Advent candle marking the dates from December 1 to 24.

The story of Christmas

The story of Christmas begins 2,000 years ago, at a time when the Roman empire ruled the land of ancient Israel.

A girl called Mary was planning to marry Joseph, a carpenter. Before the wedding an angel appeared to Mary and told her that God would cause her to become pregnant and give birth to a son. The angel also told Mary that her son would be called Jesus, the Greek form of the Hebrew Joshua, which means 'The Lord saves'.

Also, the angel spoke to Joseph in a dream, telling him that this was all true.

▼ This model shows the story of the birth of Jesus. Many people set up statues and models like this during Advent.

Shortly before Jesus was born, the ruler of Rome issued an order that everyone must go to their home town to be counted in a CENSUS. So Mary and Joseph travelled to Bethlehem, which was Joseph's home town. Mary gave birth soon after they arrived in Bethlehem, but the town was so crowded that Mary placed the baby Jesus in a MANGER, because there was nowhere else to put him.

That night, in the fields outside Bethlehem, some shepherds were watching their flocks. An angel appeared to them and told the shepherds to go to Bethlehem, where they would find a baby in a manger. The angel told them that this baby was the SAVIOUR.

The shepherds hurried to Bethlehem and found Mary, Joseph and the baby, just as the angel had said.

Twelve days after Jesus was born, a group of educated and wealthy men from the East arrived in Bethlehem. They had read that a new star in the sky means a new king has been born. When they saw a new star in the sky, they followed it to Bethlehem.

These wise men gave Jesus gifts of gold, frankincense and myrrh. In ancient times, these things were only given to kings.

Advent calendar

During the 40 days of Advent, Christians prepare for Christmas in many different ways. One way is by using an Advent calendar to learn the story of Jesus' birth.

An Advent calendar counts down the days from the start of Advent to the birth of Jesus at Christmas. The calendar might have little doors or windows, and one is opened each day. Behind the door may be a treat, a picture or information about a part of the Christmas story.

Holly and wreaths

People also prepare for Christmas by decorating their homes and churches with holly and other evergreen plants. The evergreens are a reminder of eternal life with God. Holly is prickly, so it also reminds Christians of the crown of thorns that Jesus wore on his death.

Nativity plays

Another way that Christians learn the story of Jesus' birth during Advent is by putting on a play about Jesus' birth, called a **NATIVITY PLAY** (nativity means birth).

Carols

Christians also prepare for Christmas by thanking God for sending Jesus to Earth. This is a happy time, so one way to thank God is by singing happy songs called carols, both in church and outside.

▲ The thorns on the holly are a reminder of the crown of thorns Jesus was made to wear before his death. The red berries are a reminder of Jesus' blood.

▼ An Advent calendar may be used as a fun way to help count down the days before Christmas.

If you listen to the words of many traditional carols, you can see that they are really about the ideas of hope and joy that Jesus is coming. In many churches, carols are sung during Advent worship services.

Notice that some carols, such as *O come, o come Emmanuel,* are sung only during Advent, they are not Christmas carols.

Helping others is another way to prepare for Christmas. By helping other people, Christians remember that Jesus came to Earth to help everyone.

▶ This Advent song is sung by Christians to show their hope that Jesus will come soon to save the world. EMMANUEL, Rod of Jesse, and Key of David are all other names for Jesus Christ. This song mentions Israel because Christians believe that Jesus was sent by God to fulfil ancient Jewish prophecies, which said that one day God would send a son to save the world.

O Come, O Come, Emmanuel

O Come, O Come, Emmanuel
And ransom captive Israel
That mourns in lonely exile here
Until the Son of God appears

Rejoice! Rejoice! Emmanuel
Shall come to thee O Israel

O come, Thou Rod of Jesse, free
Thine own from Satan's tyranny
From depths of hell thy people save
And give them vict'ry o'er the grave

Rejoice! Rejoice! Emmanuel
Shall come to thee O Israel

O come, O Dayspring, come and cheer
Our spirits by thine Advent here
And drive away the shades of night
And pierce the clouds and bring us light

Rejoice! Rejoice! Emmanuel
Shall come to thee O Israel

O come, Thou Key of David, come
And open wide our heavenly home
Make safe the way that leads on high
And close the path to misery

Rejoice! Rejoice! Emmanuel
Shall come to thee O Israel

O come, O come, Thou Lord of might
Who to thy tribes, on Sinai's height
In ancient times did'st give the law
In cloud and majesty and awe

Rejoice! Rejoice! Emmanuel
Shall come to thee O Israel

Christmas

This holy day celebrates the birth of Jesus Christ.

The Christmas holiday marks the end of the holy time of Advent. Christmas is a time to celebrate the day that Jesus was born. This is a very joyous and happy day.

The most important part of the Christmas holiday is Christmas Day. In churches, there is a special worship service at midnight.

Many churches are decorated in white and gold. These colours remind worshippers that Jesus is King. Worship services may include singing Christmas carols and lighting candles. Worshippers and friends wish each other a "Merry Christmas".

▲ Christmas celebrations may include worship services (far left and below), decorating an evergreen tree and giving gifts (left) and nativity scenes (above).

Nativity scenes

Many churches and families may put up statues that show the Holy Family and the manger with the baby Jesus in it. These are a reminder of the story of Christmas and of how Jesus was born in a manger in Bethlehem. These are called nativity scenes.

Christmas Day

On Christmas Day, families gather at home to have a special meal and open presents. Giving presents is a reminder of how God gave everyone the gift of his son. The gifts are also a reminder of the gifts that the wise men brought to the baby Jesus (gold, frankincense and myrrh).

Weblink: www.CurriculumVisions.com

▼ This nativity scene shows the baby Jesus being visited by the wise men twelve days after his birth, on Epiphany.

The Twelve Days of Christmas

If you think back to the story of Christmas (pages 8 to 9) you can see that the story does not end on the day Jesus is born. Instead, the Christmas story includes the visit of the shepherds and the visit of the wise men, twelve days after Jesus' birth. So, the Christmas holiday does not end on Christmas Day, but lasts until twelve days after Christmas Day, on January 5. This period of time is sometimes called the Twelve Days of Christmas.

St Stephen's Day

During the Twelve Days of Christmas, there are other holy days. One of these is St Stephen's Day, on December 26.

St Stephen was the first Christian to be killed for his faith. One way that Christians celebrate St Stephen's Day is by giving money to the poor and to charity.

In the UK, St Stephen's Day is on the same day as Boxing Day, which is not a Christian holiday. But Boxing Day takes its name from the tradition of opening church alms boxes and giving the money to the poor on the day after Christmas.

Epiphany

The season of **EPIPHANY** begins thirteen days after Christmas, on January 6. The day before Epiphany is also called Twelfth Night.

Different Christmas dates

In some Christian traditions, Christmas Day is celebrated on a different day. This is because these churches use an older calendar, called the Julian calendar, which is 13 days behind the calendar that we use. So, in these traditions, Christmas Day is January 6 and Epiphany is January 18.

Epiphany celebrates four things: the day that the wise men came to visit the baby Jesus; the day that the adult Jesus was baptised by John the Baptist; the day that Jesus performed his first miracle – changing water to wine at a marriage feast in Cana; and the coming of the Light of God into the world. Each of these events showed that Jesus was more than just an ordinary person.

For some Christians Epiphany lasts for only one day, for others it lasts until Candlemas.

Candlemas

Forty days after December 25 is February 2. This marks the end of the season of Epiphany, also called the season of Light. The candles are put out after Mass.

▲ This stained glass window shows the adult Jesus being BAPTISED by John the Baptist.

Weblink: www.CurriculumVisions.com

Lent

This is a time to get ready to celebrate Easter.

Just as Advent is a time to prepare for Christmas and the birth of Jesus, so Lent is a time to prepare for Easter, to remember the death of Jesus by CRUCIFIXION and the resurrection of Jesus. Lent begins 40 days before Easter (not counting Sundays).

Lent is a time for PENITENCE. Penitence means 'to feel sorry for any bad things you may have done'. During Lent Christians repent bad habits which have crept in, and try to change them, which often involves giving up things they like. So, some Christians do not eat any meat, chicken, eggs, dairy foods, sweets or crisps during Lent.

▼ In some countries, carnivals, parties and celebrations take place the day before Lent begins.

Shrove Tuesday

The day before Lent begins is sometimes called Fat Tuesday, Mardi Gras (which is French for Fat Tuesday), Shrove Tuesday or Carnival (the word Carnival means 'to take away meat').

For many Christians, this is a day of celebration before they begin fasting for Lent.

◀ Making pancakes is a Shrove Tuesday tradition for some British Christians.

It is celebrated in many places with parades, costumes, dancing, and music.

In the UK, many people eat pancakes on this day. Making pancakes is a way to use up all the eggs, milk and butter that are not supposed to be eaten during Lent.

Ash Wednesday

On the first day of Lent some Christians put ashes on their foreheads. The ashes stand for **REPENTANCE** and mourning. Because the first day of Lent is always on Wednesday, this day is called Ash Wednesday.

Passion plays

Lent is also a time to learn about the death and resurrection of Jesus. Many people learn about this by attending plays, called **PASSION PLAYS**, which act out the story of Jesus' death and **RESURRECTION** (you can learn more about this on the following pages). They are called passion plays because one meaning of the word passion is 'suffering'.

When people watch passion plays, they are reminded of the suffering of Jesus and this helps them to feel closer to Jesus and to God.

Worship services during Lent also include talks or sermons about the meaning of Jesus' death and resurrection.

The most important part of Lent is the last week, called Holy Week.

▼ These actors are putting on a passion play during Lent.

Weblink: www.CurriculumVisions.com

Holy Week

The last week of Lent is called Holy Week. During this week Christians remember all of the things that happened to Jesus on the week before and after he died on the cross.

To understand the whole idea of Lent, you have to think about the story of the crucifixion and the resurrection.

► Remembering the death of Jesus on the cross is at the heart of Holy Week worship.

▼ These people are carrying crosses in a procession to remember the last days of Jesus, when he was crucified.

The story of Holy Week

Jesus decided that he would spend the Jewish holiday of Passover in Jerusalem. On the Sunday before Passover Jesus and his disciples entered Jerusalem. Jesus was riding on a donkey. When Jesus entered Jerusalem, his followers placed palm leaves on the ground in front of him and shouted "Hosanna" which means 'save us'.

On Monday, Tuesday and Wednesday, Jesus preached and spoke to his followers in Jerusalem.

On Thursday, Jesus and his disciples celebrated the Jewish holiday of Passover with a special meal. Before the meal, Jesus washed the feet of his disciples. During the meal, Jesus blessed the bread and handed it to his disciples, saying, "Take this and eat it, for it is my body." Then Jesus blessed the wine and passed round his cup, saying, "Drink this, it is my blood."

After the meal, Jesus and his disciples went to pray in the Garden of Gethsemene.

While he was praying, Jesus was arrested.

On Friday morning, Jesus was taken to the Jewish high priests, who accused him of insulting God, which was a crime punishable by death.

Jesus was then taken to the Roman governor, Pontius Pilate. Pilate did not want to kill Jesus, so he offered the crowd who had gathered the choice of freeing Jesus or another man, a murderer. But the high priests convinced the people to choose the other man and Jesus was sent to be crucified.

Jesus was led away by soldiers, who beat him and put a crown made of thorns on his head. Then he was led through the streets of Jerusalem to a small hill. There he was nailed to a wooden cross and left to die.

After he died, Jesus was taken down from the cross and placed in a tomb. Early on Sunday morning, Mary Magdalene, one of Jesus' first followers, arrived at the tomb. Then, Jesus spoke to her – he had been brought back from the dead by God. This is Easter Sunday.

XIV Jesus is placed in the sepulchre.

Weblink: www.CurriculumVisions.com

Maundy Thursday

Thursday of Holy Week is called Maundy Thursday. This celebrates the day that Jesus ate the Passover meal with his followers. This meal is also called the **LAST SUPPER**. In some churches, the vicar or priest washes the feet of the worshippers. This remembers when Jesus washed the feet of his disciples.

In the UK, the Queen gives out money on Maundy Thursday to senior citizens (one man and one woman for each year of the Queen's age) who have done service to their community.

In most churches, worshippers who have been baptised take **HOLY COMMUNION** on this day. During Holy Communion, a blessing is said over bread and wine and then worshippers share the bread and wine. This is a ceremony that remembers when Jesus shared bread and wine with his disciples and told them the bread was his body and the wine was his blood.

▲ This painting shows Jesus entering Jerusalem with his disciples in the week before his death.

Celebrating Holy Week

Christians celebrate and remember some of the days of Holy Week with special services and other events in church.

Palm Sunday

The first day of Holy Week is called Palm Sunday. This celebrates the day Jesus rode into Jerusalem and his followers put palm leaves on the ground in front of him. Today, many churches are decorated with palm leaves on this day.

▼ During the Holy Communion ceremony, wine is drunk as a reminder of when Jesus shared wine with his disciples on Passover.

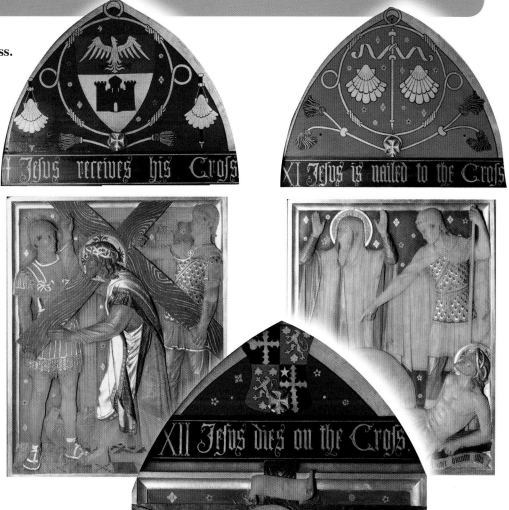

▶ Three of the stations of the cross.

Good Friday

Friday of Holy Week is called Good Friday. Good Friday remembers the day of Jesus' arrest, trial, crucifixion and burial. It is a sombre day of reflection and repentance. It is called 'good' because Jesus was our **SAVIOUR**.

In some churches there are plaques or paintings showing fourteen things that happened to Jesus while he walked on his way to be crucified. These plaques or paintings are called the Stations of the Cross. On Good Friday worshippers might walk from station to station, singing hymns and listening to the story of Jesus' death.

Holy Saturday

This is the last day of Holy Week. It remembers the day Jesus' body was in the tomb after his death and before he was resurrected. This is the last day of Lent. In ancient times, this was the day when people were baptised into the Christian faith, showing that they were beginning a new life with Christ.

Weblink: www.CurriculumVisions.com

Easter Sunday

This is the celebration and remembrance of Jesus' resurrection.

Easter Sunday is the first Sunday after the first Full Moon in spring (this is in March or April).

Easter remembers and celebrates the resurrection of Jesus after his death on the cross.

Jesus' resurrection

On Good Friday, Jesus Christ died on the cross. After his death, Jesus' body was taken down from the cross and buried in a cave. The tomb was guarded and an enormous stone was put over the entrance, so that no-one could steal the body.

On the Sunday after Jesus' death, Mary Magdalene, one of his followers, arrived at the tomb. She was amazed to see that the stone had been rolled away from the tomb. When she went inside, she saw that Jesus' body was missing. Seeing this, Mary began to cry. Suddenly, she looked up and saw two angels, who asked her why she was crying. "Because they have taken my Lord away," she told them.

As she spoke, Mary turned around and saw a man standing behind her. Mary asked the man if he knew where the body had gone and the man said, "Mary, it is I." The man was Jesus, risen from the dead.

Over the next 40 days, Jesus spoke to many of his disciples. Finally, Jesus gathered all of the disciples together. Jesus told them that they would receive help from God to spread his teachings around the world.

Then Jesus was lifted up into Heaven. This day is called Ascension Day.

◀ Singing in celebration at an Easter service.

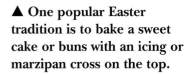

▲ One popular Easter tradition is to bake a sweet cake or buns with an icing or marzipan cross on the top.

◀ This statue shows Jesus after the resurrection – notice the marks on his hands where he was nailed to the cross.

23

Weblink: www.CurriculumVisions.com

Celebrating Easter

Worship services for Easter Sunday actually begin at sundown on Saturday.

This night-time worship service is called the Easter vigil service. The idea of the Easter vigil service is for Christians to wait and watch for the return of Jesus.

In some churches, the service begins outside the church, where worshippers gather round a fire. A very large candle, called an Easter candle, may also be lit, and worshippers may hold smaller candles during the service. The candles stand for the light of God that Jesus brought into the world. During this part of the service prayers are said and special hymns may be sung.

During the worship service on Easter Sunday, parts of the Bible that tell the story of how God created the Earth, and of how God saved the Jewish people from slavery in Egypt, are read out loud. The readings remind people of God's promise to be with them always.

Worship on Easter Day is a joyous time when Christians remember the miracle of the resurrection and of Jesus' teachings.

▼ Worshippers hold candles during the Easter vigil service as a reminder of the light of God.

Celebrating at home

At home, some people celebrate Easter by giving gifts of decorated eggs. The eggs stand for new life. Some people also give gifts of sweets during Easter. This is a reminder of the sweetness of Jesus' teachings and of the resurrection.

Families may eat a big meal at home to celebrate. Lamb is a popular food to eat at this meal. This is because Jesus is sometimes called 'The Lamb of God', reminding us that lambs were killed at the Jewish Passover, as he was. In the UK, hot cross buns are also eaten throughout the Easter holiday.

▲ Hot cross buns are a popular Easter treat.

◄ An Easter egg decorated with a drawing of Mary.

▼ Chocolate eggs are a reminder of both the sweetness of Jesus' teachings and of new life.

Pentecost (Whitsun)

Pentecost, popularly known as Whitsun, marks the beginning of the Christian church.

Pentecost takes place 50 days after Easter Sunday. Pentecost began on the day of the Jewish festival called Shavuot, or the Feast of Weeks.

In ancient times this Jewish festival celebrated the spring harvest and Jews still celebrate Shavuot as a holy day.

Today, Christians celebrate Pentecost as the day that God appeared to the disciples in the form of the **HOLY SPIRIT**.

How Pentecost began

After Jesus rose up into Heaven, the disciples were confused and were not sure how they should follow Jesus' instructions to teach God's word.

A short time later, the disciples were gathered together to celebrate the holiday of Shavuot (remember, the disciples were all Jewish). Suddenly, a sound like a mighty wind was heard rushing through the room where they were

▲ This painting shows the disciples on Pentecost. You can see a small flame flickering above each of their heads.

gathered. Over the head of each disciple flickered a small flame. This was a sign that God was with them. The disciples found that they could speak and understand any language and could work miracles.

One of the disciples, Peter, began to preach to a crowd that had gathered to celebrate Shavuot.

He told the crowd that they should be baptised in the name of Jesus Christ. Many people came forward to be baptised. This was the start of the Christian church.

From this day on, the disciples preached and spread the message of Jesus and the Christian church began to grow.

Weblink: www.CurriculumVisions.com

Celebrating Pentecost

In the UK, Pentecost is also called Whitsun. The word 'whit' comes from the word 'white', recalling the white clothing of those who are baptised at Pentecost. Sun stands for Sunday. So, Whitsun means 'white Sunday'.

Pentecost is a happy and joyous festival. Ministers in church often wear red robes. The colour red stands for the flames that appeared over the heads of the disciples. Worshippers may wave ribbons and flags to remember the wind of the Holy Spirit.

Worship services include readings, songs and sermons about the Holy Spirit. Because this was the day when the first Christians were baptised, many adults choose to be baptised into the Christian faith on Pentecost. Some churches also go on a 'march of witness' to show their community that they believe in Jesus and his teachings. There may also be church festivals or fêtes, to celebrate that the Christian church began on Pentecost.

For some churches, such as Pentecostal churches, this is one of the main holidays of the year. These churches may have very big worship services on Pentecost, with hundreds of people being baptised at the same time.

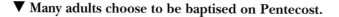

▼ Many adults choose to be baptised on Pentecost.

▼ On Pentecost, ministers and priests may wear red robes, or robes with flames on them, as a reminder of the flames that appeared over the heads of the disciples.

Harvest festival

There are many other days of celebration throughout the Christian calendar. One of the most popular is the harvest festival.

Harvest festivals are usually celebrated after the autumn harvest, in September or October. There is no fixed day for this.

This is a time to thank God for the gift of food, and for the gifts of sun, rain and earth that make it possible for us to grow food.

Celebrating harvest festival

There are many ways to celebrate the harvest festival. The festival is usually very colourful. Worshippers may decorate the church with autumn leaves, fruits and vegetables, and bring different kinds of foods into the church.

Worship services include singing hymns such as *We plough the fields and scatter, Come ye thankful people, come* and *All things bright and beautiful.* These hymns remind worshippers to be thankful to God for making the world and everything in it.

After the worship service, people may share the foods of the season by having a fête, a party or a meal together.

Weblink: www.CurriculumVisions.com

Giving to others

Because the harvest festival reminds Christians of all the good things God gives them, this is also a time to share these things with others. So, in schools and in churches, people bring food from home to the harvest festival service. After the service, the food that has been put on display is usually made into parcels and given to people in need.

We plough the fields and scatter

We plough the fields and scatter
The good seed on the land,
But it is fed and watered
By God's almighty hand:
He sends the snow in winter,
The warmth to swell the grain,
The breezes and the sunshine,
And soft, refreshing rain.

All good gifts around us
Are sent from heaven above;
Then thank the Lord,
O thank the Lord,
For all his love.

He only is the maker
Of all things near and far;
He paints the wayside flower,
He lights the evening star;
The winds and waves obey him,
By him the birds are fed;
Much more to us, his children,
He gives our daily bread.

We thank thee then, O Father,
For all things bright and good,
The seed time and the harvest,
Our life, our health, our food.
Accept the gifts we offer
For all thy love imparts,
And what thou most desirest,
Our humble, thankful hearts.

Weblink: www.CurriculumVisions.com

Index

Curriculum Visions is a registered trademark of Atlantic Europe Publishing Company Ltd.

First published in 2007 by
Atlantic Europe Publishing Company Ltd
Copyright © 2007 Earthscape

The right of Lisa Magloff to be identified as the author of this work has been asserted by her in accordance with the Copyright, Designs and Patents Act 1988.

All rights reserved. No part of this publication may be reproduced, stored in a retrieval system, or transmitted in any form or by any means, electronic, mechanical, photocopying, recording or otherwise, without prior permission of the Publisher and the copyright holder.

Author
Lisa Magloff, MA

Religious Adviser
Reverend Colin Bass, BSc, MA

Senior Designer
Adele Humphries, BA

Acknowledgements
The publishers would like to thank the following for their help and advice:
St James Church, Muswell Hill, London;
St John the Baptist Church, Wightman Road, London; Father George Christidis of St Nictarios, Battersea, London; Rector Father Terence Phipps of St James Church, Spanish Place, London; the Covenant Players.

Photographs
The Earthscape Picture Library, except:
(c=centre, t=top, b=bottom, l=left, r=right)
pages 3, 4tl, 8–9, 10t, 13tr, 14, 15, 16b, 18, 20br, 23, 24, 25, 26, 30–31 *ShutterStock*;
pages 26–27 *Alamy*; page 28 *Art Directors/TRIP*.

Illustrations
David Woodroffe

Designed and produced by
Earthscape

Printed in China by
WKT Company Ltd

Christian holy days
– *Curriculum Visions*
A CIP record for this book is available from the British Library
ISBN: 978 1 86214 500 9

This product is manufactured from sustainable managed forests. For every tree cut down at least one more is planted.

Dedicated Web Site
There's more about other great Curriculum Visions packs and a wealth of supporting information on world religions and other subjects at our dedicated web site:
www.CurriculumVisions.com